T0194874

THE CONSEQUENCE
TURNING YOUR LIFE AROUND

Victor Akinyemi

WESTBOW
PRESS®
A DIVISION OF THOMAS NELSON
& ZONDERVAN

WestBow Press books may be ordered through booksellers or by contacting:

WestBow Press
A Division of Thomas Nelson & Zondervan
1663 Liberty Drive
Bloomington, IN 47403
www.westbowpress.com
844-714-3454

ISBN: 978-1-6642-5333-9 (sc)
ISBN: 978-1-6642-5334-6 (e)

Print information available on the last page.

WestBow Press rev. date: 12/23/2021

To everyone who desires a great change
and impact in their lives.
To you, who may be reading this book right now.
To those who are on the verge of giving up, feeling frustrated,
suffering several failures, or losing hope for a better life.
To those who are facing the negative consequences
of their decisions and actions.
To everyone who desires to help others
achieve greatness in life.

CONTENTS

ACKNOWLEDGMENTS

I am grateful to God Almighty from whom all wisdom comes. I will forever be grateful to God for His mercy, faithfulness, and leading me to write this book.

I am grateful for the inspiration and wisdom of the men and women of God for the impartation I enjoyed and benefited from by listening to their recorded messages, reading their books, or learning under their leadership.

I am eternally grateful to God for the supernatural connection to meet my mentor, teacher, pastor, and spiritual father, Pastor Sam Adeyemi, the senior pastor of Daystar Christian Centre. He trained and impacted me for more than two decades. He is blessed with uncommon wisdom and knowledge. His teachings and leadership have been tremendous blessings to my family and me. God led me to him twenty-eight years ago as a teenager, and I served under his ministry until God moved me to start another ministry. I am very grateful to his wife, Pastor Nike Adeyemi, for her courage and love and seeing us become great blessings for others.

I am deeply grateful to my wife, Janet Oluwakemi Akinyemi, and our daughters—Oluwabukunmi, Oluwapelumi, and Oluwanifemi—for their courage, love, tolerance, and endurance.

May God bless you all.

INTRODUCTION

All actions and decisions have consequences in life. We all make choices every day; some may be well thought through, and others may be more impulsive. Some decisions are easy, and others are complex.

How we manage the challenging times matters a lot when rediscovering ourselves.

This book is about looking at how our decisions and actions—both past and present—can determine what our futures look like. The consequences of our actions and decisions can be positive or negative.

This book shows how we can focus on the positive sides of every person, despite their flaws, mistakes, and failures. Every person who is considered terrible was once a very good child or a nice and responsible person. This person has the potential to be more responsible and positively affect many lives if they are embraced with love and determination by good people.

This book focuses on how to turn our worlds around irrespective of who we used to be and how people see us. It helps us work toward becoming better people. Every creature has great potential for success and greatness, depending on the side of them we choose to touch or see. "The stone which the builders rejected has become the chief cornerstone" (Psalm 118:22 NKJV).

Positive consequences help turn lives around for better impact and development. Consequences are what happens after behaviors, decisions, and actions. Consequence can be positive or negative.

Positive consequences confirm good behavior and positive actions. The focus of this book is on positive consequences and helping those who may be going through negative consequences become better and improve their environments for good.

CHAPTER 1

YOU WILL FINISH WELL

Of the sons of Issachar who had understanding of the times,
to know what Israel ought to do, their chiefs were two
hundred, and all their brethren were at their command.
—1 CHRONICLES 12:32 (NKJV)

Since the beginning of creation, God has determined there
will be times and seasons. If there is a time and a season for
everything under the sun, it is our responsibility to find out in
prayers what God is saying about our new season.

Just as the natural human can observe a season changing
from summer to winter or hot to cold, the spiritual human
can see and understand the change of seasons in the spiritual
realm.

When we study the Word and receive the Holy Spirit, the
spirit is enlarged and alerted to the changing seasons. Satan

attempts to tamper with our times and seasons because he knows that if a set time is changed, visions, dreams, and supernatural conceptions can be aborted.

God ordained times and seasons, and He expects us to understand them in every season to know what we are supposed to be doing in every season. Our success is determined when we know what God expects from us in a particular season:

> And He changes the times and seasons, He removed kings and raised up kings, He gives wisdom to the wise and knowledge to those who have understanding. (Daniel 2:21 NKJV)

Thank God for the season you are in right now:

> He has made everything beautiful in its time. Also He has put eternity in their hearts, except that no one can find out the work that God does from beginning to end. (Ecclesiastes 3:11 NKJV)

God shows us the end, but He often does not show us what we will pass through to get to the end and fulfill the vision. That is why He is God.

God is in control of everything, including the season you feel is unfavorable. He has not forgotten you, and He will not forsake you. Every time and season you are in is working in your favor.

I see you rising above what seems to be an unfavorable time and season in Jesus's name. His hands will preserve you, you will rejoice, and everything shall turn out for your good in Jesus's name.

> He found him in a desert land And in the wasteland, a howling wilderness; He encircled him, He instructed him, He kept him as the apple of His eye. (Deuteronomy 32:10 NKJV)

The Lord is watching over you. You're special to Him. There is nobody exactly like you. You are fearfully and wonderfully made. Don't allow the world to redefine you against who God says you are. They will always be wrong.

They see your weaknesses, but God sees your strengths. They see your failures, but God called you a success. Who will you choose to believe?

You will rise and shine. Go for the best, lead others, and succeed where others fail. May the Lord cause your light to shine always.

You have the ability—and you have what it takes to finish strong. Your past and present experiences are meant to improve your position in life. Your academic failures, your economic failures, and your weaknesses are not meant to destroy you; they are meant to reposition you as a candidate for success.

People have failed often in the past and succeeded later in life because they saw themselves as successes and not failures.

Different seasons come our way in life, but the choice to succeed is a personal decision, and that is what I encourage you to do.

There is a turning point for people when God transforms their lives. A negative person has the opportunity to become a positive person by deliberately changing the people they associate with. Make yourself available for counseling, join a prayer group, and study your Bible every day.

Grace will always meet you where you are, but it will never leave you where it found you. Enjoy that grace always.

> As iron sharpens iron, so a man sharpens the countenance of his friend. (Proverbs 27:17 NKJV)

> For the Word of God is living and powerful, and sharper than any two-edged sword, piercing even to the division of soul and spirit, and of joints and marrow, and is a discerner of the thoughts and intents of the heart. (Hebrews 4:12. NKJV)

> He who walks with wise men will be wise, But the companion of fools will be destroyed. (Proverbs 13:20 NKJV)

Failure is not a sign of weakness. It's a choice! Success is not a sign of being strong; it is a personal choice. You're better positioned to be a success after several failures in life.

> For I know the thoughts that I think toward
> you, says the Lord, thoughts of peace and not of
> evil, to give you a future and a hope. (Jeremiah
> 29:11 NKJV)

Your personal experiences when you tried frequently and failed remain part of your learning experiences that will equip you for better performance when you become successful. They are not a waste of time. If you tried several times and failed, it's not proof that you're a failure. It is proof that you have not discovered what works for you.

> And do not be conformed to this world, but be
> transformed by the renewing of your mind, that
> you may prove what is that good and acceptable
> and perfect will of God. (Romans 12:2 NKJV)

The world is waiting to celebrate your contributions to the development of humankind. Your past mistakes and failures are giving way to your success. You're a success and not a failure; many are waiting for you to lead and direct them. Some of these people will avoid the pitfalls of your past by learning from your experiences. Your mentorship will give them the boost, the courage, and the speed to achieve success. This makes the circle and production of true success faster, leading to improvements and developments in your life.

Finishing strong is a choice, and it is a worthy choice to make if we want to turn our world around.

> I press on toward the goal for the prize of the upward call of God in Christ Jesus. (Philippians 3:14 NKJV)

> Being confident of this very thing, that He who has begun a good work in you will complete it until the day of Jesus Christ. (Philippians 1:6 NKJV)

> Do you not know that those who run in a race all run, but one receives the prize? Run in such a way that you may obtain it. (1 Corinthians 9:24 NKJV)

Count it a great privilege if you're among the few who are affecting our world for good in any area. God has given you the grace to function and contribute to the development of our world.

Some people have not smiled for a long time, but the impact and contributions you make bring smiles to their faces. Your impact is not small. That is all we need to make the difference in our world.

> Look at the birds of the air, for they neither sow nor reap nor gather into barns, yet your heavenly father feeds them. Are you not more value than they? Which of you by worrying can add one cubit to his stature? (Matthew 6:26–27 NKJV)

Speak to the giant in you. You're more than this.

Lord, meet the needs of everyone who calls upon Your name. Let peace and joy fill their hearts in Jesus's name.

Let God have everything in your life, and you will never have to worry about anything in life.

I speak grace into your life in Jesus's name.

Thank You, Lord.

CHAPTER 2

YOUR SEASON OF DISCOVERY FOR GREATER IMPACT IS NOW

Opportunity doesn't really announce itself as opportunity; it is usually disguised in challenges.

Think about it. Gold would never be gold if it did not endure fire to bring out its best quality. Its greatest value lies in the challenge of going through the fire.

Your ability to discern helps you to spot opportunities and be comforted in your season of challenges. Such opportunity never showed up during your comfort season; otherwise, you may not see it, but it is aimed to launch you into a glorious season.

Don't give up on that situation or challenge. You're likely very close to your opportunity and breakthrough.

I see you breaking forth and returning with your testimonies in Jesus's name. You will be great.

> Wisdom is the principal thing; Therefore get wisdom. And in all your getting, get understanding. Proverbs 4:7 (NKJV).

Don't let your position dictate who you are; your position is only temporal. Let your personality define your position. If you're ever afraid of leaving that position to do what God has called you to do next, it's proof that your position is dictating who you are. Until you leave, you may not discover the great opportunities that lie ahead.

You occupy that position to solve problems; the position is not solving the problems. Human beings solve problems; their positions do not solve problems. This is why we have different people occupying the same position at different periods but with different capacities for solving problems.

Anytime you see an organization or a country that is poorly managed, it has nothing to do with the positions occupied by individuals. It has a lot to say about the incompetence and characters of individuals who have failed in delivering efficient, effective, and quality service.

There are many problems in organization and countries, but God has given humans the capacity and the wisdom to solve those problems. If individuals or countries fail, they fail because they lack the wisdom of God.

People will only remember you for the problems you solved but not the positions you occupied over a given period of time. Your position is irrelevant.

Stand for justice and righteousness and always be upright. Enjoy the uncommon grace to make an impact in the lives of people who come across your way in life in Jesus's name.

Everyone has been created beautifully and is designed with a specific purpose. Certain actions taken in the course of time may lead to the discovery of that purpose—even when those actions were taken with a wrong motive.

> And we know that all things work together for good to those who love God, to those who are the called according to His purpose. (Romans 8:28 NKJV)

If you have a strong feeling not to embark on a journey but end up going on the journey, the journey could result in a fatal accident. Instead, graciously, your life was saved.

The consequence of your action is not about the accident; it is about what you learned from the experience. God preserved you for a purpose. You're in a position to share your experiences with others on the importance of listening to your mind and being sensitive to your inner spirit. That automatically changes your perspective about your life. What God did for you by preserving your life is greater than the consequences of your disobedience.

Some women were pregnant as teenagers—even though it was against their wishes. It looks as if the negative consequence of their misdeeds will haunt them forever, but their children became a source of joy after many years. Many of these young women tried to get pregnant years after getting married, but they did not have an opportunity to get pregnant again. The consequences of their actions were only a temporary setback as teenagers, but God has a big reason for allowing it. They now have feelings of joy for those children who were once the reason for their sadness because they felt they had made terrible mistakes in the past.

Positive consequence come from actions that you like or enjoy. When used correctly, positive consequences will increase the frequency of positive behaviors.

Sometimes, negative consequences turn out to be positive consequences. Many people who turned out well and became influencers in different areas of their lives were once people with negative consequences. Those negative consequences led them to meet the positive-minded people who influenced their lives, and they later became people of influence. Today, they are also impacting lives positively.

Saul was once a negative person, but when he had an encounter with Christ, he became a positive person. He became Christ's disciple and led thousands of negative-minded people to Christ. His life is still a great blessing to millions of Christians—even after his death.

There is great hope for negative-minded people. Even those whose lives are extremely dangerous can be helped if we recognize that they are God's creature and believe that God can touch their lives and use them to be great blessings to others.

When we focus on their strengths and not their weaknesses, we can help them rediscover themselves and turn away from their negative attitudes.

A negative person is someone whose lifestyle, beliefs, or way of life does not add meaningful value to their immediate environment and the people who come their way. Their flaws and weaknesses are considered setbacks,, and they have limited chances for success in life.

These negative people have great potential and gifts that can be tapped and turned into huge blessings. There are no ugly creatures of God, and no one is weak or a failure because everything and everyone created by God is very good. They will bring out the best they're created for if we focus on their strength and potential.

> Then God saw everything that He had made, and indeed it was very good. So the evening and the morning were the sixth day. (Genesis 1:31 NKJV)

> For every creature of God is good, and nothing is
> to be refused if it is received with thanksgiving.
> (1 Timothy 4:4 NKJV)

Lazarus was dead and buried, but Jesus saw that he was not dead as people thought. He saw potential in him, and He saw that he had more to give his family and his environment. Jesus woke him up from sleep—sorry, from death—because there was something about him that could still bless humanity.

We cannot afford to write off anyone and conclude that their negative past is the final story about their lives. God can still use them—no matter our feelings and understanding of their negative pasts. The consequences of their actions may be negative, but they still have futures ahead of them that can be very positive. They need our help, and we cannot abandon them if we believe they still have hope.

People who have abundant thoughts live abundant lives. The key to abundance is meeting limited circumstances with unlimited thoughts.

People who lead abundant lives realize that their results are an expression of their thinking. If they don't like their results, they change their thoughts. The thoughts you habitually think create your circumstances, situations, and conditions. For example, if you're constantly thinking about success, you will start to see elements of success in your life. A certain amount of constriction or limitation is associated with a scarcity-based thoughts. Express gratitude for the abundance you currently have, and you will begin to experience more of it in your life. It is through your thoughts and responses that you cultivate and display greatness.

There is enough abundance for everyone. No one is kept in poverty by shortness in the supply of riches. There is more than enough for everyone.

People with an abundant mindsets see the world as a win-win proposition. They are genuinely happy for the success, well-being, achievement, recognition, and good fortune of other people. They go out of their way to help others and contribute to their greatness because in doing so, they believe we can all achieve more.

People with abundant mindsets operate from a strong sense of self-worth. They know the results they see—or don't see—in their lives are a direct representation of how they feel about themselves. They believe that if they want to transform their dreams into reality and create lives they love living, it is important to see themselves as someone who is 100 percent worthy of living their dream life and capable of creating it. They're able to generate new opportunities and possibilities for themselves and their lives much more easy than others may be able to.

To shift yourself into abundant mindset, you must first embrace the truth that we live in a truly abundant world. Infinite intelligence has countless ways to bless you. It may not always feel this way when you're experiencing scarcity, lack, or a setbacks, but it's true.

Your source of abundance is life itself.

Sometimes, a change in circumstances will cut off one channel, but if you look carefully, you will find another one appears in its place. If someone takes a breath, there isn't less air available for the next person. Abundance works in the same way.

We live in an abundant, giving universe, and you were meant to give too.

If you want love and abundance in your life, give it away.

When you're always focused on what you can get, you're always on a "get frequency," which is a frequency of scarcity and lack.

We live in an abundant, giving universe, and when you practice being generous, using generous thinking and language, you don't need to worry about getting because the frequency of your thoughts is one of increase.

I have seen how moving from one country to another can be a spiritual leading. The experience in the new country can be very depressing, and they think about going back to where they came from. Relocation feels like the worst decision ever made, even when they are sure that God led them to the new country. The negative experience during the few years in that country leads them to move to another country. This was also a spiritual leading.

Sometimes, we think our first destination is our final home where God wants us to settle, but we may be wrong. In this case, you're not sure if your movement to another country will be a positive one or not, especially when both countries are considered developed nations. God asking you to relocate to a particular country does not mean that it is your final country. He's taking you there to fulfill His purpose in your life. It may just be the beginning of a journey on your way to the best place or country He has planned for you. That does not mean the first country you migrated to is a bad country—some still prosper in that country—but because you have not reached the final destination He plans for you, you may not achieve your life's purpose until you move to the next country or the place where your full blessings are waiting for you. Life can be very cheap and fulfilling if we follow God's lead.

Fortunately, the new country might bring a big relief to the family—far more than the first developed country they migrated to. The family had the benefits of living in what can be considered a developed nation. They had work permits and good jobs, they lived comfortably, and all medical care was free. A few years down the line, they obtained their permanent residency. God suspended the laws of the country in their favor due to a crisis that engulfed the nations of the world. They worked in the health sector, and the government passed a law to issue permanent residency to all the people who worked during the pandemic but did not have permanent residency.

Circumstances and events can lead people to where they will be favored. You might call it a coincidence, but it is not. Not everyone who migrated to the country was given such privileges or enjoyed such divine favors. They took certain steps and actions, and they were responsible for their actions even though they did not know if the consequences of their actions would be positive or negative.

There are divine occurrences in our lives. We might think something is going to be negative, but it eventually turns out to be positive. What about if that family who had refused to move when prompted to move to another country? They could have said the risk was too much to bear. They could have abandoned the thought when they did not qualify to stay in any of the countries beyond a certain period of time. They were not qualified to obtain work permits to earn a living. They could have given several excuses. Situations might have been worse for them if they did not make the move because the future was very uncertain.

The spiritual controls the physical. You may not appreciate the inner mind that is leading you until it finally leads you to a place of rest and peace if you choose to obey your inner spirit mind. It is good to follow your heart and remain committed to your spiritual leading.

The opportunities the family enjoyed don't happen frequently in life, including the laws of a nation being suspended to favor a very few. The experience of the family will change their perspectives about life, which may impact generations after them, especially for families who migrated from countries with underdevelopment, corruption, nepotism, and no value for life.

Most times, the consequences of our actions are not seen

as positive developments in disguise. However, over time, we begin to see the positive impact of what seem like negative actions leading to a fulfillment of purpose.

Life should not be seen from a negative perspective—no matter what pain is experienced. There is always a purpose and a reason why God takes us through different experiences in life.

Don't wait for the perfect timing for what you need to do now. That perfect time does not exist; it may just be your imagination. God does not work with our timing.

No one achieved greatness in life by waiting until things took shape. You work to make things better; things don't get better by waiting and doing nothing. Your decision and actions create what you see.

Stop procrastinating, take a step to start that business or project now, and touch someone's life in a positive way. As you carry it, help will come in unexpected ways. If it's not going to work out, it will surely lead you to a discovery of what works for you. You were chosen for something great.

Not doing anything at all shuts the door of discovery and greatness. Until you step out, nothing is going to happen—and you may not know if it's achievable.

Step out in faith and see God in action.

You will be great.

If the journey is far, it can't be farther than God. He sees the end from the beginning.

He has showed you the great future, and He alone can take you there. Don't be discouraged; He will not leave you alone.

Everything He said concerning Joseph, He fulfilled. Joseph went through a tough time, but he was not alone. God was with him. From prison, he went to a palace and became the second most powerful man in Egypt after Pharaoh. It was part of the package to greatness.

You will also be great if you can endure the season and put your trust in Him. Your God-given dream will surely come to pass.

You will be great.

CHAPTER 3

THE INFLUENCERS OF DECISIONS AND ACTIONS

Fight the good fight of faith, lay hold on eternal life,
to which you were also called and have confessed the
good confession in the presence of many witnesses.
—1 TIMOTHY 6:12 (NKJV)

There is no irreversible case with a Bible-based faith. To keep your faith going, you must keep hope alive. You are not a loser; you are a winner.

Somebody is taking delivery of a long-awaited promise of God. You were almost given up, but God has delivered the promise by His power. Praise God!

Don't give up; you're already there. God is putting the finishing touches on your case. Your testimony will be great.

21

You may have been mocked, but it's your turn to be celebrated. Thank Him because He has done it.

Congratulations.

There are many things that influence our decisions and actions in life. Some of these are products of habits we formed over a period of time. They shaped and formed our decisions. Some of them are not products of deep thoughts—even though it is required—but we care less about the outcome of such decisions. These decisions build negative momentum over a period of time, possibly years after years, and they start impacting our lives negatively.

I will be glad to share three of these influencers with us.

1. Culture

And do not be conformed to this world, but be transformed
by the renewing of your mind, that you may prove what
is that good and acceptable and perfect will of God.
—ROMANS 12:2 (NKJV)

Culture can be described as the characteristics and knowledge of a particular group of people, encompassing language, religion, social habits, music, and arts. It can also be seen as the growth of a group identity fostered by social patterns unique to the group.

Culture revolves around religion, food, clothing, language, marriage, music, beliefs, and behaviors. Culture is also the driver of decisions, actions, and the overall performance of individuals.

Religion and social beliefs impact the pattern of our decisions and actions most of the time. Some people have developed the wrong conception that money is the root of all evil. This misconception, over a period of time, can place a limit on financial freedom for some people. This is a misconception.

> For the love of money is a root of all kinds of evil, for which some have strayed from the faith in their greediness, and pierced themselves through with many sorrows. (1 Timothy 6:10 NKJV)

Money is not the root of all evil. Money is a means for the exchange of goods and services. If money was the root of all evil, as some claimed, money would not be accepted as a means of exchange. Life would be meaningless without the presence of money—physical cash or not.

Many have been held captive and are not able to enjoy life as God intended for them because of their wrong and negative beliefs.

Life should be looked at from a positive perspective. The positive mind created the world we live in.

> The earth was without form, and void, and darkness was on the face of the deep. And the Spirit of God was hovering over the face of the

waters. Then God said, "Let there be light, and there was light." (Genesis 1:2–3 NKJV)

There is potential for light in darkness. Until you see possibility in every impossibility, you may not be able to enjoy life to the fullest.

The consequences of our actions and beliefs can make life very interesting if we focus on our hidden positive potential instead of what we perceive as the negative result of our actions.

It is good to note that every culture that runs contrary to the Word of God cannot bring development to the people and the nation at large. Any culture that does not embrace love, peace, kindness, and holiness will always run against itself. The Word of God is the standard way of life.

The consequence of darkness brings disaster to everyone, but the consequence of light brings joy, illumination, and victory over the entire world and all creation, including animals and every living thing.

2. Value System

Pray for the peace of Jerusalem: "May they prosper who love you. Peace be within your walls, Prosperity within your palaces."
—PSALM 122:6–7 NKJV

Let us pray for the nations of the world. Neglect, abandonment, corruption, greed, and mediocrity have brought our nations to their knees. Only lifting our voices to God for mercy can stop the sweeping hand of God.

Guard yourself with the Word of God every day and pray. The voices of the people have reached up to heaven. God is merciful. He can deal with the situation without bloodshed in the land, but for the wicked, there is no hiding place. God love His creatures and despises wickedness in His people.

Lord, have mercy on the nations of the world and restore all that the devil has stolen in the land in Jesus's name.

A value system is the hierarchy of values that all moral beings have, which is a reflection of their choices. Values are important because they influence perception. Integrity, respect, responsibility, servant leadership, trust, honesty, honor, and justice are reflected in our daily lives, and to a large extent, they determine what we accomplish in life.

The consequences of who we turn out to be in life—our decisions and actions—are anchored to this value system. If our choices and values are wrong, we need to redefine our values in order to command positive consequences.

Understanding these values and establishing a shared value system removes stress and uncertainty from our lives.

Values are important because they influence perception. They lay the foundation for the understanding of attitudes and motivation.

The values are established by our parents, teachers, friends, and others. Our value systems may get altered as we grow up and are exposed to other value systems. Values are a person's or a society's beliefs about good behavior and what things are important. Values are collection of guiding principles— what one deems to be correct and desirable in life—especially regarding personal conduct.

3. Association, Friends and Family

Settle it with God today. No man ever saw His
glory without first seeing the vision. What do you see?
You will be great. The righteous should choose his friends
carefully, For the way of the wicked leads them astray.
—PROVERBS 12:26 (NKJV)

Association is a group of people organized for a joint purpose. It is an association of people with a common purpose and a forward structure.

Do not be deceived: "Evil company corrupts
good habits." (1 Corinthians 15:33 NKJV)

It is very likely that members of different associations may be influenced negatively or positively based on the beliefs and cultures of the association, even when the beliefs place the members in conflict with their personal beliefs and values. This will likely happen when members join the association based on certain benefits and motivations. In such instances, achieving their personal purpose may be in conflict with the association's purpose, thereby having consequences on the lives of individual members.

> A man who has friends must himself be friendly,
> But there is a friend who sticks closer than a brother. (Proverbs 18:24 NKJV)

The same thing may apply to friends and family. The choice made by a person in a given family or friendship may lead to consequences the person may live with for years. Some friendships and family values can be toxic and detrimental to achieving positive consequences in life.

Every individual is responsible for their actions in life. The emphasis of this book is to focus on how individuals can leverage the strength of positive individuals. What you make your habits over a period of time will form a pattern or lifestyle that can predict who you will turn out to be in life.

You cannot give what you don't have, but if you must fulfill a great purpose in life, there are ways and patterns that guarantee positive consequences. You can learn from individuals who have positive influences in life. The ultimate way is to abide in the Word of God, which is the most important, develop a personal relationship with Christ, and trust in Him that you will finish strong.

A family is the bedrock upon which the foundation for positive influences began. Not every family can be entrusted with such an important foundation. Sometimes what is lacking in a family can be learned from friends and associates who share credible values.

Spending more time with the people who are nice and good helps you develop positive consequences. It is natural for a positive-minded person to associate with another positive-minded person. The product of such relationships produces a better and healthier association and friendship. Remember, some relationships can be destructive.

> He who walks with wise men will be wise,
> But the companion of fools will be destroyed.
> (Proverbs 13:20 NKJV)

> As iron sharpens iron, So a man sharpens the countenance of his friend. (Proverbs 27:17 NKJV)

CHAPTER 4

HOW TO TURN YOUR LIFE AROUND

This is why it is said: "Wake up, sleeper, rise from the dead, and Christ will shine on you. Be very careful, then, how you live—not as unwise but as wise. Making the most of every opportunity, because the days are evil."
—EPHESIANS 5:14–16 (NIV)

Whenever a new year passes, time passes. A new year gives us the opportunity to redefine our priorities, purpose, lives, and vision and reestablish worthwhile goals.

Paul was talking to people who were sleeping through life.

Nothing will change if you're not committed to changing things by yourself.

You need to arise and let Christ shine upon you. Is there

anything you want to do differently this year? You need to desire it, be passionate about it, and be committed and dedicated to it.

Redeeming the time means getting back everything you have lost in the past year. This year must be a year that you will redeem the time.

Find out what is the will of God for your life, and you can stop wasting your time, your energy, your gifts, and your talents.

Let the will of God dictate your schedule and the kind of people you will keep company with. It's okay to leave people because you're not supposed to be with everybody. Not everyone will be happy with your success and determination. Remember if you do anything that will distract your focus, you're destroying your time.

Any bad habit that controls your life is a time stealer. You can't allow anything to control your purpose and life again.

Your life is your time, and whatever you do with your time is your life. Anyone or anything that controls your time is consuming your life. The secret to protecting your time is knowing your purpose.

I prophesy over you today that this year will be a year of great fulfillment in your life. You will arise and shine above your contemporaries in Jesus's name. I see giants rising from here today because you believe in this message.

> And do not be conformed to this world, but be
> transformed by the renewing of your mind, that

you may prove what is that good and acceptable
and perfect will of God. (Romans 12:2 NKJV)

1. Be a better person each day.

So it was, when he had turned his back to go from Samuel,
that God gave him another heart, and all those signs came
to pass that day. When they came there to the hill, there
was a group of prophets to meet him, then the Spirit of
God came upon him and he prophesied among them.
—1 SAMUEL 10:9–10 (NKJV)

Saul he was from the smallest of the tribes of Israel and his
family had was the least of all the families of the tribe of
Benjamin. God favored him in spite of his lack of qualifications.

My God is not partial. He blesses whom He choose to
bless. I prophesy over you today that your disqualification has
become your qualification. God will set aside laws, rules, and
policies to announce you for divine favor because the Spirit of
the Lord will come upon you.

When you come in contact with prophets this year, you
will also prophesy. Everything you have lost in the past will
gladly be announced to you that it has been found. You will go
up with God to high places and be highly favored. You will sit
in the place of honor among those who matter, and the Lord
will give you another heart. All these signs will come to pass
in your life in Jesus's name.

Turning your life around involves challenging yourself every day, going a step better than yesterday, and embracing change. You're not too old to make a significant change in your life—no matter the failures of the past. You can set a new goal for yourself and be determined to achieve the goals. Become a better version of yourself each day.

> Commit your works to the Lord. And your thoughts will be established. (Proverbs 16:3 NKJV)

> I can do all things through Christ who strengthens me. (Philippians 4:13. NKJV)

2. Pay attention to your health.

If you want to live long enough to witness the change you desire. Only the living can achieve their goals and experience the change they want. Exercise and eat healthier foods—and you will have enough strength and energy for each day.

> Beloved, I pray that you may prosper in all things and be in health, just as your soul prospers. (3 John 1:2 NKJV)

> A merry heart does good like medicine, But a broken spirit dries the bones. (Proverbs 17:22 NKJV)

3. Practice time management.

Turning your life around entails spending your time efficiently. Time management is key. Value your time and place priorities on what you do with your time. Don't be a time waster. Your action today is a reflection of how your tomorrow will be.

> See then that you work circumspectly, not as fools but as wise. (Ephesians 5:15 NKJV)

> Redeeming the time, because the days are evil. (Ephesians 5:16 NKJV)

4. Develop a culture of saving.

Financial burdens can be very heavy and may lead to many problems. Changing your financial situation without a culture of saving may not be realistic. Start saving from your paycheck if you want to see a wealthy financial future. Consistency in your savings can help turn your life and future around.

> The rich rules over the poor, and the borrower is servant to the lender. (Proverbs 22:7 NKJV)

> He who has a slack hand becomes poor, but the hand of the diligent makes rich. (Proverbs 10:4 NKJV)

He who gathers in summer is a wise son. He who sleeps in harvest is a son who causes shame. (Proverbs 10:5 NKJV)

5. Learn a new skill.

Think big! You don't achieve big things by accident. Have the curiosity to execute and keep moving forward. If you fall, you will rise again. Believe in your dream—you can start now. Surround yourself with those who believe and can help preserve your dream. Run away from dream killers. Don't let others define your limits. Money is not a show of success; some have it but lack wisdom and leadership. The positive effect you have on people is most valuable. You can make it happen. I see you arising and doing great exploits for God and the people in Jesus's name.

Learning a new skill presents additional opportunities. Find out what new skill can add value to you. This may change your perspective toward life and create a new future for your financial freedom.

Do you see a man who excels in his work? He will stand before kings; He will not stand before unknown men. (Proverbs 22:29 NKJV)

In everything give thanks, for this is the will of God in Christ Jesus for you. (1 Thessalonians 5:18 NKJV)

Signs and wonders become our natural experience when thanksgiving becomes our way of life. We thank God for what we have seen, and we thank Him for what we want to see.

> Jesus said, "take away the stone. Martha, the sister of him who was dead said to Him, Lord, by this time there is a stench, for he has been dead four days."
>
> Jesus said to her, "Did I not say to you that if you would believe you would see the glory of God?"
>
> Then they took away the stone from the place where the dead man was lying. And Jesus lifted up His eyes and said, "Father I thank you because you have heard Me."
>
> "And I know that you have always hear Me, but because of the people who are standing by I said this, that they may believe that You sent Me."
>
> Now when He had said these things, He cried with a loud voice, "Lazarus, come forth"
>
> And he who had died came out bound hand and foot with graveclothes, and his face was wrapped with a cloth. Jesus said to them, "Loose him and let him go. (John 11:39–44 NKJV)

Everyone saw the dead Lazarus and concluded that there was no hope that he would live again. The living God saw a living Lazarus, and that became a reality for all to see.

Lazarus came forth, and he became a living being because that was what Jesus saw. What do you see?

As you thank God for the things He has done—and for the things you want to see Him do in your life—I see God stepping into your case, giving you victory, healing your disease, breaking down the barriers, and giving you testimonies in Jesus's name.